A Small Group Discussion Guide

Tame your FEARS

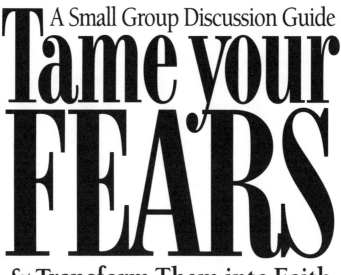

& Transform Them into Faith, Confidence & Action

NAVPRESS

BRINGING TRUTH TO LIFE
NavPress Publishing Group
P.O. Box 35001, Colorado Springs, Colorado 80935

OUR GUARANTEE TO YOU

We believe so strongly in the message of our books that we are making this quality guarantee to you. If for any reason you are disappointed with the content of this book, return the title page to us with your name and address and we will refund to you the list price of the book. To help us serve you better, please briefly describe why you were disappointed. Mail your refund request to: NavPress, P.O. Box 35002, Colorado Springs, CO 80935.

The Navigators is an international Christian organization. Our mission is to reach, disciple, and equip people to know Christ and to make Him known through successive generations. We envision multitudes of diverse people in the United States and every other nation who have a passionate love for Christ, live a lifestyle of sharing Christ's love, and multiply spiritual laborers among those without Christ.

NavPress is the publishing ministry of The Navigators. NavPress publications help believers learn biblical truth and apply what they learn to their lives and ministries. Our mission is to stimulate spiritual formation among our readers.

ISBN 0-89109-761-9

Some of the anecdotal illustrations in this book are true to life and are included with the permission of the persons involved. In some cases, names and identifying details have been changed to protect the privacy of the people involved. All other illustrations are composites of real situations, and any resemblance to people living or dead is coincidental.

Printed in the United States of America

3 4 5 6 7 8 9 10 11 12 13 14 15 / 02 01 00

FOR A FREE CATALOG OF
NAVPRESS BOOKS & BIBLE STUDIES,
CALL 1-800-366-7788 (USA)
OR 1-416-499-4615 (CANADA)

CONTENTS

INTRODUCTION

Fear is one of our oldest and deadliest enemies. It causes illness, stifles creativity, prevents love, destroys families, depletes energy, and causes addictions. For women, fear is often an unwanted constant companion. In this study, we will chart the development and defeat of fear and provide a framework for using fear as a stepping stone to humble faith, renewed confidence, appropriate power and courage, and trusting reverence for a sovereign, powerful, and loving God.

Each session contains the following sections:

Warm-up: The questions in this section are designed to get you thinking about the topic to be discussed that day. Sometimes the first question will ask you to share insights gained since the previous session.

Text: This material is adapted from the book *Tame Your Fears* (NavPress, 1993). You can decide as a group if you want to read the text before or during each session. Reading the book is not necessary for successfully completing this study, but for a more in-depth look at the topics discussed you will enjoy a leisurely reading of *Tame Your Fears.*

Questions: These questions will help you to unmask and analyze five fears with which women struggle: (1) The Fear of Things That Haven't Happened . . . Yet!, (2) The Fear of Being Vulnerable, (3) The Fear of Abandonment, (4) The Fear of Truth, and (5) The Fear of Making Wrong

5

Choices. The questions will lead you through a constructive, biblically based method for dealing with your personal fears. You don't have to read these questions before the group time, although doing so will add to what you will be able to contribute to the discussion. The leader of your small group may choose not to discuss some questions if time is limited.

Think About It: A study involving the sharing of deep, long-term fears is highly personal in nature. Therefore, some of the deepest reflection is emphasized in the "Think About It" sections, which are meant for private contemplation. If you are studying with a group, you do not need to discuss the questions raised in these sections together.

Looking to God: Each session will provide an opportunity for prayer focused on praise and thanksgiving—as well as on concerns, fears, and spiritual struggles that surface during the small group meetings. Some women may elect to pray silently while others will choose to pray aloud.

Into Our Lives: This section has applications for living out the aim discussed in each session. You should do one of these activities each week. This will not require a lot of time, and the activity will add to the session's impact on your life. Insights from this section will sometimes be shared at the beginning of the following session.

For Meditation: This section contains quotes to stimulate additional reflection and personal application pertaining to the aim in each session. These quotes can be used during the discussion or later for individual consideration.

For Memorization: Choosing a constructive resolution for your fears will be easier with an ever-increasing knowledge of God's Word. Each week you will have a suggested Scripture verse to memorize, helping you to internalize the truth you have discussed.

HOPE . . . WHEN LIFE GETS SCARY

Fear: Defining the Paralysis

WARM-UP

1. If you are meeting with a group, give your name and then describe the room in your house or apartment where you feel the most peaceful, safe, and relaxed. Share why you enjoy spending time there.

WHAT ARE YOU AFRAID OF?

I was controlled by fear for most of my life. For a while, public speaking was one of my paralyzing phobias. At other times I was afraid of potential disasters that *might* happen—especially to a family member I loved. I was always afraid of losing control, and I was panicked by the fear of disappointing people and then facing rejection or abandonment.

The more I talked to other women, the more I knew I wasn't alone. I talked to women who were afraid of any kind of change. Others were paranoid about facing their past mistakes or immobilized by the fear of confronting their past victimization by other people. Many of the women I met were afraid of lost opportunity because of the choices they made to marry (or not marry), or to take

7

(or not take) certain jobs. Some were afraid of losing their confidence in God and also afraid to tell their doubts to anyone. Most of these women faced the fear of success and/or failure at some time in their adult lives.

Experts tell us there are only two fears we are born with: falling and loud noises. All other fears are *learned* or *acquired*. So where does fear come from? Most of us believed that our faith in Christ would bring contentment, peace, and joy. But we also expected another benefit—the absence of fear! So when we still feel fear, we are often embarrassed to tell anyone and we usually feel like spiritual failures!

2. In your own words, how do you define the word *fear*?

3. Have you ever had a friend you felt comfortable sharing your deepest fears with? If so, describe some of the characteristics of that friend.

UNDERSTANDING FEAR

There are basically three types of fear: *holy* fear, *self-preserving* fear, and *slavish* fear. The first comes from our reverence for and awe of the God who created us and loves us. The second has everything to do with the God-given instinct to run from danger, avert an accident, or protect ourselves and those we love. This wise form of fear causes us to take responsibility for ourselves and others. It provides the motivation to teach our children to look both ways before crossing the street and to use caution on a bicycle.

This study, however, is about slavish fear—the negative type that kills expressions of love, plugs lines of communication, imprisons victims of abuse, taunts with ridiculous phobias, controls by manipulation, and erodes all confidence and security. *Wise, self-preserving fear shifts into slavish fear when it becomes obsessive and controlling.*

4. How would you rate your struggle with fear on a scale of 1 to 10? One means, "Fear is not a problem for me, and it never has been." Ten means, "I've struggled with fear for most of my life, and at times it paralyzes me."

1	2	3	4	5	6	7	8	9	10
Freedom from Fear						Paralyzing Fear Problem			

5. What is one of your earliest memories of being afraid? If it's not too personal, describe that fear to the group.

WHERE DOES FEAR COME FROM?

Boiled down to the bottom line, the negative aspect of fear is a problem of *focus* and *self-reliance*. It all began in the Garden of Eden. Adam and Eve had known a perfect relationship with God. They knew Him as their creator, companion, teacher, and friend. At this time in history the only fear present was absolutely holy. There was purity in God's relationship with Adam and Eve.

After Adam and Eve disobeyed God, a change occurred. With no additional instruction, Adam had an instant awareness of slavish fear. When God called out to Adam he responded, "I heard you in the garden, and I was afraid because I was naked; so I hid" (Genesis 3:10). Instead of rushing to be with his best friend, Adam now doubted his position, fearful of not being accepted, and hiding in the bushes.

The false roots of Adam's fear are still with us today. God had always been there for him, but self-reliance kept him from asking for help:

▼ Adam feared abandonment, yet chose to abandon the One he needed the most.
▼ He feared disclosure, yet needed to be honest with God to learn how to live in a fallen world.
▼ He was ashamed of revealing who he really was, yet could not begin to function normally without disclosure.
▼ He made himself lonely because he feared rejection.
▼ He gave in to temptation and felt unforgiven and afraid.

When sin entered the human race, Adam's *focus* had been off God and *self-reliance* kicked in—and Adam was running and hiding.

Slavish fear is a natural consequence of self-reliance. Sometimes "helping myself out and doing my best in the middle of my fears" keeps me from admitting that *sin and self-reliance are the same thing.* Trusting in self as Adam did leads to shame, slavery, obsessive behavior, and self-protection. It becomes a learned cycle that is hard to break.

WHAT HAPPENS INSIDE MY HEAD WHEN I'M AFRAID?

What really happens inside my head when I'm afraid? When we analyze the whole process, it's easier to understand as a chain reaction:

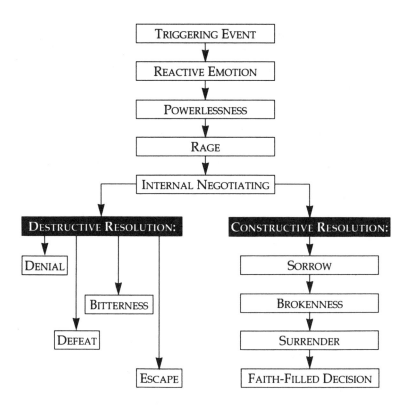

Triggering event/situation/person: Something or some-one is always the cause of fear. There is a "trigger point" that makes us aware of danger, evil, or pain. The cause might be from a real or imagined source, but it feels threatening, harmful, and disarming.

6. What "trigger points" produce a fearful response in you?

Reactive emotion: Our first honest reaction to the triggering event is virtually involuntary. It might be the emotion of shock, terror, panic, dread, anxiety, horror, hurt, anger, or shame. One person might have a panic reaction that is immediately recognizable as fear. Someone else's first response might be anger, which could be displayed by a volatile outburst or by passive, wounded withdrawal.

7. With your personality, what type of emotional response to fear are you most likely to demonstrate? Circle the descriptive words in the above paragraph that best describe your normal reaction. Share your "key words" with the group and feel free to make a comment.

Powerlessness: After we have an automatic emotional response to an event, it doesn't take long to realize that things aren't going according to our plan. We feel alone and unprotected before a scary, powerful person or situation. We are not in control the way we would like to be or thought we were. This is frightening, and we don't feel comfortable staying with it for long. Our natural tendency is to try to regain control, so we move to the next stage.

Rage: The rage response sometimes begins with a feeling of betrayal. "Wait a minute, here. What happened to my safety and security? How can this be happening to me? I can't believe *that person* or *life* or *God* has let me down so completely!" Sometimes we raise our fist in the face of God and cry, "I hate what is happening here and *I won't have it!* I refuse to feel helpless and dependent. I can't trust You any more. I'm determined to find a better way to resolve my feelings." This rage response may or may not feel like anger, but in essence, it's a posture of defiance (self-reliance) that is based on the fear that God can't be trusted and we must go it alone in order to have things the way we want them. This is the nature of sin.

Internal Negotiating: Here lies the turning point in the chain reaction. The first four steps in the process occur very quickly—almost involuntarily. But once we have (1) identified a trigger point, (2) experienced a reactive emotion, (3) felt totally powerless, and (4) responded with demonstrative or internal rage, we begin (5) *internal negotiating.* We try to come up with a way to "fix" our feelings or situation. It's our self-centered, determined effort to escape both our pain/powerlessness and the need to surrender to a power greater than ourselves. At this pivotal point, we come up with our options: Will we choose the path of self-reliance or the path of God-reliance? Depending on our answer, we will "resolve" our fear in either a destructive (God-denying) way or a constructive (God-honoring) way. One of the two following courses of action will be chosen.

THE DESTRUCTIVE COURSE OF ACTION

If we choose the destructive route, we'll get stuck in one of four "resolutions." None of these choices solves the problem or takes away the fear. They are rigid, dead-end alternatives.

Denial: A frequent reaction to fear is to deny there is a problem, person, or painful situation that must be dealt with. Even when our initial reactions to a triggering event are powerful, we are amazingly adept at climbing up to the surface of life again where we can pretend we aren't really angry or afraid.

Defeat: Many of us respond to fear with a posture of automatic defeat. We believe negative things have happened to us, causing our fears, and we have no power to change our feelings or life situations. We have no energy or confidence to take action and believe we can't handle our triggering event, situation, or person—so we give up.

Bitterness: Another popular response to fear is to look around and find someone else to blame. It might be our parents, friends, coworkers, or even God. If we can point the finger at another person who is responsible for causing our grief, we can "justify" our paralyzing bitterness and delay any positive action toward resolving the fear in a God-honoring way.

Escape: Perhaps the most prevalent of all the destructive resolutions to fear is running away from reality. Many of us have become quite skilled at muffling our troubles in layers of compulsive/addictive behavior so we don't have to admit our feelings or deal with our fears. This God-denying choice leads to perfectionism, legalistic spirituality, workaholism, codependency, or enslavement to a wide variety of mood-altering substances or behaviors.

8. Circle the destructive choice you are most likely to make in the middle of a fear-producing situation. If it's not too personal, share your response with the group.

Denial   Defeat   Bitterness   Escape

THE CONSTRUCTIVE COURSE OF ACTION

If we choose the constructive route, we allow our rageful, self-reliant thrashing around to bring us to our knees— and into a more honest, substantial relationship with God.

Sorrow: Sometimes we wallow around in a mental pigpen of betrayal, powerlessness, hurt, and anger for a long time. The turning point occurs when we stop trying to "fix" our feelings or situation and begin to grieve honestly and deeply. We live in a groaning creation where imperfect people hurt and disappoint us. That's sad. When we are abandoned by someone we expected to love us, that's sad. But when we allow the sorrow of a fallen world to penetrate us, something happens. When we cease playing the blame game and allow ourselves to grieve, we change.

Horrible as it is, it is the first major step toward a real solution. We have been betrayed. That's sad. We have felt powerless. That's sad. We have been profoundly hurt. That's sad. We've been angry and internally consumed with rage. That's sad. We aren't relating to other people and God the way He intended His children to relate.

14

That's sad. But Christ promised that those who mourn will be comforted!

Brokenness: We are needy people. When we deeply acknowledge that we are much too impotent and unwise to resolve our problems and fears without help from a power much greater than ourselves, we are on our way to real healing. We can continue to respond with fearful emotions while we're walking on the uncertain waters of life. Or we can recognize the strength of the hand He is already extending toward us and humbly acknowledge our need. It's saying, "Lord, I cannot pick myself up by my own bootstraps. I need You." A broken heart is a humble heart, and a humble heart isn't too ashamed or self-reliant to ask for help.

Surrender: Surrender is knowing where to turn and doing it. It implies giving up my will. My desires. My plan of action. My fearful disguises. Taking off my masks. Revealing my need. Confessing my sin. With my surrender comes a willingness to be taught. It's crying, "Father, save me! I'm drowning in my circumstances. My fears envelop me. Uncertainties are everywhere. My past is a ghost before me. Father, forgive me for thinking I could solve all this on my own. Take away any false guilt I carry for the honest feelings of hurt or anger I have had or for what others have done to me. Help me to toss my extra baggage overboard. Teach me how to trust You."

Faith-filled decision: Once I let go of the situation, the person, the deep emotion of fear, and the potential consequences and implications—placing it all in God's hands—I can decide to trust Him to take me through whatever lies ahead. I can face my past and accept the truth. I can reveal who I am to others and not be overwhelmed with shame or anxiety.

LOOKING TO GOD

9. Meditate on 2 Timothy 1:7 (KJV): "God hath not given us the spirit of fear; but of power, and of love, and of a sound mind." We know slavish fear

15

is not from God. Take a moment to ask Him to help you to look honestly at your fears and the way you respond to them during this study. Ask Him to reveal any problem you might have with *focus* and *self-reliance*. If He has already revealed any sin in your life, confess it to Him.

INTO OUR LIVES

Overcoming lifelong fear is inconvenient. It viciously destroys carefully constructed facades. It leaves one feeling naked, unprotected, vulnerable, and exposed. But instead of feeling ashamed or threatened by our fears, we can choose to stop our destructive course of action and learn how to process our fears in a way that will involve God in the process. In His hands fear can be a stepping stone to humble faith, renewed confidence, appropriate power and courage, and trusting reverence for a sovereign, powerful, and loving God.

10. a. Take a few minutes to list your deepest fears. They could involve family members, situations, events, past experiences, mistakes, or personal anxieties.

   b. Look back at pages 13-14 and reread the choices involved in a destructive course of action. Next to each of your fears, write down any of the words that apply to the way you have responded to your fears (denial, defeat, bitterness, or escape, for instance).

c. Reread the constructive course of action on pages 14-15. Choose one of your fears and prayerfully consider a God-honoring way of responding to this threatening situation/person/event. Write out your thoughts.

11. a. Read Matthew 14:22-33 What were the uncertain circumstances the disciples faced?

b. What wrong conclusion did they arrive at?

c. Peter yelled out a desperate call, "Lord save me!" Think of a time in your life when you felt that desperate.

d. There was immediate calm because Jesus reached out to him "without delay" and said, "You of little faith . . . why did you doubt?" Why do you think many of us don't experience this immediate calming connection with God in the middle of our overwhelming fears?

e. Do you agree or disagree with this statement: "The opposite of fear is faith"? Explain.

The text portions of this session were adapted from chapters 1 and 2 of *Tame Your Fears*. Read these chapters on your own for a more in-depth look at the topics discussed.

FOR MEDITATION

The Bible says, "perfect love drives out fear" (1 John 4:18). It's in the Bible and it's true. But how does it work? Does that verse mean *we* are to love *perfectly?* That's impossible! Perhaps the answer lies in *God's perfect love for us which casts out slavish fear and allows us to enjoy a happy life, free from the bondage of the past.*

"In love," John says, "there can be no fear,
for fear is driven out by perfect love.
Fear has to do with punishment and anyone who is afraid
is still imperfect in love" (1 John 4:18).
Have you learned to think of the Father as the judge,
the spy, the disciplinarian, the punisher?
If you think that way, you are wrong.
The Father's love is revealed in the Son's.
The Son has been given to us that we might give up fear.
There is no fear in love.[1]
BRENNAN MANNING

Fear is primarily a response to power.
It indicates a desire to flee. In contrast to anxiety,
fear generally has a specific object. . . . Fear can have either
a positive or a negative impact . . .
[it] can be the antithesis of faith
or a part of faith. It is the antithesis of faith
when it is directed toward circumstances rather than God.
It is a component of faith when it moves us
to trust in and submit to Him.[2]
DR. FRANK MINIRTH, DR. PAUL MEIER, AND DON HAWKINS, Th.M.

To get the most out of this study, set a specific time to meet with God this week. Tell Him about your deepest fears and your most painful memories. He will not judge you or embarrass you. He longs to lift you out of the

18

uncertain waters of fear and give you the security of His compassionate, affirming grip of faith.

FOR MEMORIZATION

Write the following verses on an index card and place it where you will see it most often this week. (Try putting it on the visor of your car, on your desk, on your kitchen window sill, or on a visible mirror in your home. Read it often until it becomes a part of your memory bank and your belief system.)

For God hath not given us the spirit of fear;
but of power, and of love, and of a sound mind.
2 TIMOTHY 1:7 (KJV)

Have I not commanded you?
Be strong and courageous. Do not be terrified;
do not be discouraged, for the LORD your God
will be with you wherever you go.
JOSHUA 1:9

NOTES
1. Brennan Manning, *The Ragamuffin Gospel* (Portland, OR: Multnomah Press, 1990), pages 74-75.
2. Frank Minirth, M.D., Paul Meier, M.D., and Don Hawkins, Th.M., *Worry-Free Living* (Nashville, TN: Thomas Nelson Publishers, 1989), page 215.

OVERCOMING THE FEAR OF THINGS THAT HAVEN'T HAPPENED . . . YET!

Fear 1: Paralyzing Phobias
Fear 2: Potential Disasters

WARM-UP

1. When you think about the future, do you tend to dwell on the potential "best case scenario" or the "worst case scenario"? Why?

THE CEMETERY

The year we moved to the house next to the cemetery produced the worst memories of my childhood. My second-story bedroom window faced the burial grounds, and the scene from that spot would send chills through anyone who struggled with fear. I knew I was a Christian and that Heaven would be my final destination, but the process of dying and getting there always bothered me.

The view from the window was never pleasant, but there were two horrible times to look toward the cemetery: when the moon was bright and when a group of mourners stood by one of those big holes in the ground. I always pulled my shade down, trying to place a tangible barrier between me and all of those dead bodies outside. But sometimes I had to look. And I was terrorized!

One evening I was put to bed early. Mom and Dad

were entertaining company, and I knew I was not to interrupt the party the adults were having downstairs. I couldn't sleep and suddenly, I dared to peek out the window. The moon illuminated the entire graveyard, and macabre shadows dancing between the trees and the marble stones convinced me that something (or someone) ghastly and hideous was coming toward my window.

Quickly, I weighed the difference between my father's wrath if I interrupted the party and my total inability to live with this gripping fear alone. I had a tooth that was slightly loose, but not ready to fall out on its own yet. I knew if the tooth came out, it would earn me the right to go down the steps where there was safety from the grisly scene out my window.

I took a piece of string, tied it around my tooth, and secured the other end to the door handle. It took fierce courage to slam that door—but the desired result was forthcoming. The immature extraction took place, and my prize tooth and blood-stained pajamas earned me a ticket to the party below. And I was safe from the hideous shadows and reminders of death on the other side of my window for another night.

2. As a child, did you have an irrational or illogical fear about something that *might* happen? If so, share it with the group.

I'm convinced my mother understood the depth of my fear. In years past I had run to her side of the bed when I awoke in the middle of the night with nightmares. She always put an arm around me and let me fall asleep in her bed before Dad got up and placed me back in my own bed, long after my fears were quieted.

3. When you were growing up, who was the main person who calmed your fears? What did this individual do to quiet your anxious heart?

THE GHOSTS OF TODAY

I have often looked back on that stage of my life with a smile. My "real" fear of what might happen was based on my knowledge of the verse in the Bible that says, "The dead in Christ shall rise first." I prayed Jesus would not return before we moved to a different house. I truly believed my heart would fall out of my body if the Lord came back and I had to see those graves open. If Jesus did come for His own while we lived in that house, I hoped it would be during the daylight. Maybe I could handle the situation if I wasn't alone in my bedroom at night.

In addition to legitimate fears, children are afraid of many "unreal" ghosts, and certainly the power of imagination makes their fears far more exaggerated than any potential existing danger. But there are many days when I deal with fears that are just as debilitating as those I experienced from the bedroom window. Only this time they don't look like eerie shadows. Because I'm older and can actually identify some of the "gruesome goblins" of fear in my life, they are more obvious, and in many ways, more painful and paralyzing.

4. Often our fears are based on things that *might* happen. Place an "x" in the box in front of any of the following trigger points of fear you struggle with in your own life.

   ❏ "What if I lose someone I love? I don't know how I could go on without that person in my life."

   ❏ "What if I lose my job? The company is going to lay off more people and I just know I'll be one of them."

   ❏ "What if I'm a bad mother? How can I ever be sure I'm raising my children properly? What if they turn away from God?"

   ❏ "What if the economy falls apart? What will happen to our country?"

23

- ❑ "What if I have an accident? I've been in a wreck before and I know it will happen again."

- ❑ "What if I can't afford to pay for my children's education? People can't make a living in today's world without a university degree."

- ❑ "What if I never get married? I don't have any retirement plan and the Social Security System seems so shaky. I always thought I'd be married and financially secure by now, but I'm not."

- ❑ "What if I can't get pregnant? I want a child more than anything and every month my disappointment is deeper and I fear the worst—infertility."

- ❑ "What if my husband gets interested in another woman? He's so attractive and the women in his office flirt with him all the time."

- ❑ "What if we get transferred to another place? My whole world is wrapped up in this community. My family lives here. I have a meaningful ministry in my church. I just *can't* leave here."

- ❑ "What if I face death prematurely? I know Heaven is my final destination, but I am so afraid of the *process* of dying."

5. Which one of the above fears have you struggled with the most? Does your imagination ever add to the fear? Share your thoughts with the group.

FROZEN IN A SEA OF HOPELESSNESS

6. When a *triggering event* produces a *reactive emotion* of fear that develops into an irrational panic, it is easy to feel totally *powerless*. We then move to *rage* and

then on to *internal negotiating*. A few of the things we sometimes internalize and believe (at least for a while) are listed below. Place an "x" in front of any of the comments you can identify with regarding your reaction to past fears.

❑ "I sometimes feel totally powerless to change my fearful situation."

❑ "I know I'm supposed to trust God when I feel afraid, but that really seems like a pat 'spiritualized' answer that doesn't mean much to me."

❑ "At times I believe there is nothing I can do to alter my losing reaction to fear."

❑ "I frequently feel very angry at the person who triggers this fear in me!"

❑ "I usually refuse to dwell on my fears. If other Christians would just forget their fears and get on with their lives, they could be happy, too."

❑ "I get so mad at myself and embarrassed in front of people when I'm paralyzed by fear."

❑ "I usually wonder what God wants me to learn from the fearful situations I face."

❑ "I'm beginning to believe I can't handle my fears and I feel like giving up on trying."

❑ "I'm convinced if I had more supportive people in my life, I'd be able to let go of my fears."

❑ "I really don't ever have a problem with fear. If I work harder and get more involved in worthy causes, I'll forget my worries."

7. Which of the above "internal responses" is most typical of your response to fear? Explain.

8. "Someone once described FEAR in an acronym: *F*alse *E*xpectations *A*ppearing *R*eal. For the most part, what we fear is not real—it is merely our mind *imagining* something awful that has not yet happened."[1]
   Do you agree or disagree with that statement? Why?

   Don't worry about anything; instead, pray about everything; tell God your needs and don't forget to thank him for his answers. If you do this you will experience God's peace, which is far more wonderful than the human mind can understand. His peace will keep your thoughts and your hearts quiet and at rest as you trust in Christ Jesus. (Philippians 4:6-7, TLB)

9. a. According to this passage, what should we do with our worries?

   b. What benefits will follow if we heed God's instructions for dealing with anxiety?

   c. Give your opinion on why we continue to choose worry over trust when we say we believe the Bible.

10. Read each of the following scriptures and restate the key thought in your own words.

Deuteronomy 31:8

Matthew 6:25-27   *Matt. 7:7*

Matthew 6:34

1 Peter 5:7

11. At this point in your life, which of those verses is the most meaningful to you? Why?

12. Think about a fear you have right now that involves something that hasn't happened yet. Select one of the following destructive alternatives you could be tempted to choose in the middle of your fear. How might you respond that way?

   ▼ *Denial* (Denial deceives a person into not investigating her feelings, pain, thoughts, or motives.)

27

▼ *Defeat* (Defeat comes over us when we are so overwhelmed by what we *can't* do to change the situation or person involved that we give up.)

▼ *Bitterness* (Bitterness always looks for someone or something to blame for our pain or discomfort.)

▼ *Escape* (Escape involves covering up our fear and personal pain by running to compulsive/addictive behaviors. These escapes can look as harmless as perfectionism or as lethal as drug and alcohol dependence.)

THINK ABOUT IT
  ▼ *Life is full of negative things that might happen.* Have you faced the reality of living in a fallen world, or are you still expecting life to be easy and free of pain?
  ▼ *As long as you choose a path of personal growth, you will face fearful situations.* Have you accepted the fact that saying yes to new opportunities and challenges brings numerous fearful situations that you must deal with?
  ▼ *Acknowledging your anxieties is a positive first step.* Are you so fiercely independent that you refuse to admit you need help, or are you willing to admit your fears to God and key people in your life?

▼ *An attitude of optimism will make today more enjoyable.* Have you added one humorous thought to your life during the last twenty-four hours? (To help you get started, ponder this: "The people who tell you never to let little things worry you have never tried sleeping in the same room with a mosquito."[2])

▼ *Choosing a faith-filled decision is much less frightening than living with the underlying fear that comes from feeling helpless.* If you have developed a destructive pattern for dealing with fear, will you choose to face your problem and take progressive steps toward learning how to practice making faith-filled decisions daily?

LOOKING TO GOD

Divide into groups of two or three to discuss question 13.

13. What part of the constructive resolution for fear is the hardest for you to put into practice? (Look at the graph of the chain reaction on page 11.) How could someone pray for you?

Pray for each other regarding specific needs that were mentioned. Thank God for the victory He can give you over worry, anxiety, and fear.

INTO OUR LIVES

14. Write a letter of thanks to someone in your life who has helped you to overcome a troublesome fear, or to someone who has encouraged you during a fearful time in your life.

15. Sometime this week read Luke 1:26-38. It's the story of Mary, the mother of Jesus. She was young, engaged, and in love with a wonderful man. Then the angel came with a shocking announcement. That was her *triggering event!* Try to trace what happened to Mary in this passage, as you review the chain reaction involved in the anatomy of fear. You will notice an absence of "What ifs," and an attitude of submission to God that seems to skip some of the steps most of us have to go through to arrive at a faith-filled decision. What do you think her secret was? If time permits, write out your thoughts.

16. This week, call a member of your group and share what God is teaching you through this study. If possible, get together for further discussion and prayer.

The text portions of this session were adapted from chapters 3 and 4 of *Tame Your Fears.* You can read these chapters on your own to learn more about the topics discussed.

FOR MEDITATION

Worry is a cycle of inefficient thoughts whirling around a center of fear. . . . Worry doesn't empty tomorrow of its sorrow; it empties today of its strength.[3]
CORRIE TEN BOOM

I am an old man and have known a great many troubles, but most of them never happened.[4]
MARK TWAIN

Don't worry about the world ending today.
It's already tomorrow in Australia.[5]
BARBARA JOHNSON

Stop reading only the grim sections of the newspaper.
Watch less television and start reading more books
that bring a smile instead of a frown.
Locate a few acquaintances who will help you laugh more
at life. Ideally, find Christian friends who see life through
Christ's eyes, which is in itself more encouraging.
Have fun together. Share funny stories with each other.
Affirm one another.[6]
CHARLES SWINDOLL

FOR MEMORIZATION

Don't worry abut anything; instead,
pray about everything; tell God your needs and don't
forget to thank him for his answers.
If you do this you will experience God's peace,
which is far more wonderful than the human mind can
understand. His peace will keep your thoughts
and your hearts quiet and at rest
as you trust in Christ Jesus.
PHILIPPIANS 4:6-7 (TLB)

NOTES
1. John-Roger and Peter McWilliams, *The Portable DO IT!* (Los Angeles, CA: Prelude Press, 1993), page 42.
2. Barbara Johnson, *Splashes of Joy in the Cesspools of Life* (Dallas: Word Publishing, 1992), page 101.
3. Corrie ten Boom, *Quotable Quotations,* compiled by Lloyd Cory (Wheaton, IL: Victor Books, 1985), pages 446-447.
4. Mark Twain, *Inspiring Quotations,* compiled by Albert M. Wells, Jr. (Nashville, TN: Thomas Nelson Publishers, 1988), page 220.
5. Barbara Johnson, *Pack Up Your Gloomees in a Great Big Box* (Dallas: Word Publishing, 1993), page 117.
6. Charles Swindoll, *Laugh Again* (Dallas: Word Publishing, 1993), page 75.

OVERCOMING THE FEAR OF BEING VULNERABLE

Fear 3: Losing Control
Fear 4: Revealing Who I Really Am

WARM-UP

1. a. Where were you in the birth order of your family? Did you "boss" siblings, or were you "bossed"?

   b. In what ways do you think your position in the birth order affected the types of fears you have experienced as an adult?

2. When you think of the word *vulnerable*, what comes to your mind?

WHAT DOES THE FEAR OF BEING VULNERABLE HAVE TO DO WITH CONTROL?

Webster says the "vulnerable" person is "open to attack, hurt or injury; [capable] of being . . . wounded [either because of being insufficiently protected or because of being sensitive and tender]; liable to greater penalties than the opponents."[1]

Opening ourselves up to other people instead of controlling them means we are vulnerable to letting them hurt us deeply. We'd often rather choose a path of control, so we'd never have to open ourselves up to experience the potential pain of an honest, open relationship. We often work hard at not revealing who we really are on the inside, and we cover up our fears and true feelings with disguises and perfectionism.

3. Do you have at least one friend you can be vulnerable with? If so, how long did it take the relationship to develop? Describe the benefits of this friendship.

UNDERSTANDING CONTROL

I've always been impressed by competent women. Intelligence, confidence, and a strong commitment to the work ethic is an attractive combination. As a young married woman, I selected a few "worthy" mentors and decided to become one of the super-achievers.

"Average" was a word I loathed. When I committed myself to a task, it was done well. I enjoyed tight schedules, impossible agendas, a full calendar, and demanding opportunities. After all, I believed God was worthy of excellence—and I always felt more spiritual when I was buried in work. I wasn't sure excellence, by God's standards, was defined by an insurmountable schedule and an unrealistic workload, but godly people applauded my efforts and this only increased my desire to please them. Their affirmations and enthusiastic approval assured me I was selecting the right path.

As the firstborn of six children, being "in charge" came naturally. I was the built-in babysitter, which made me the frequent disciplinarian of my four younger sisters and one brother. Dad was the adult child of an alcoholic and had learned to "take charge" at a very young age. He valued strength, leadership, authority, personal discipline, obedience, self-control, and commitment to God. Dad taught me the following slogan: "Be a leader, not a follower; the whole world is made up of followers, but it takes a real individual to be a leader."

4. On the following scale, circle the number that best represents how controlling you are. You can share the number you circled with your group.

1   2   3   4   5   6   7   8   9   10
I dislike controlling others.   I like to be in charge.

5. Do you agree or disagree with this statement? Explain.

Control is an outgrowth of fear, insecurity and lack of self-esteem. The more anxious a woman is the more she wants to control and, conversely, the more secure a woman is the less likely she will need to control.[2]

DEFINING THE FEAR

The fear of losing control is one of the most difficult fears to recognize. Why? In its early stages it looks so appealing. Women caught in the control trap appear to be dynamic, sharp, aggressive leaders—the "movers and shakers" in our society. They get things done. Their résumés are impressive and their list of accomplishments is unending. Christian women who fit into this category are publicly honored for their commitment to worthy causes.

6. The fear of losing control wears a variety of disguises. Read through the following list, and place a check in front of any of the ten controlling identities you sometimes assume.

❏ *The manager.* This person always leads every group she participates in. She is quick to volunteer and slow to delegate because someone else might not do the job as efficiently or effectively as she does.

❏ *The manipulator.* This woman's technique is so perfected that she gets people to do what she wants and they actually believe it was their own idea. Frequently the manipulator comes from a home where one or both of her parents were dysfunctional. She learned how to manipulate difficult people and situations at an early age—just to keep the peace and have the semblance of a normal life.

❏ *The martyr.* The woman who controls situations and people "because no one else in the family will help" often becomes a martyr. Frequently, she gives up her own rights and financial resources to "sacrificially" meet the needs of others. Then, "after all she's done for them," she controls them with guilt and obligation.

❏ *The meanie.* This person knows she is a nag capable of intimidating those around her. Known for her negative attitude about everything, she wears her family down by constant criticism. She controls by her forcefulness, browbeating, and policing of activities.

❏ *The most spiritual.* Women who are married to nonChristians or "less spiritual" spouses sometimes fall into the trap of flaunting their organization of the religious training of the children in such a way that they subtly make their husbands feel like worthless, uncaring creeps for their lack of interest or involvement in church-related activities. Single women can also exhibit their "spiritual prowess" to gain control in family and church situations.

❑ *The mother of the extended family.* Women with very honorable motives often control their children far into adulthood by "protecting them from serious mistakes" or "helping them to make right choices." Sometimes she assumes the decision making related to family reunions, care of elder parents, and coordination of all birthday parties and special events. She thinks she's doing it because no one else cares as much as she does. Later she resents being left with all the work and responsibility.

❑ *The most perfect person.* The most subtle disguise of all is perfectionism. For the Christian woman, it appears to be "excellence," which always has a pat on the back and a word of affirmation attached. The perfectionist has trouble with fatigue—there are never enough hours in a day to get everything done properly.

❑ *The mime.* The possibly humorous disguise is nonverbal control. This woman is not a "screamer"— but she has powerful control over the people in her life by a certain look in the eye, the raising of an eyebrow, a grimace, or a body-language signal understood only by another family member.

❑ *The mask of illness.* Some have learned to control by exhibiting physical or emotional problems. When a woman is ill, she becomes the center of attention. Family members change their plans in order to be close to her in "her hour of need."

❏ *The main attraction.* An insecure woman often learns how to control men by her feminine charm. Afraid of intimacy, this woman controls men by her looks and childlike flirtation, but fear keeps her from developing a meaningful relationship with anyone.

7. Share with the group the controlling disguise you wear most often.

THE HIGH WALL OF PROTECTION

For years my fear of vulnerability was hidden behind a mask of false confidence. If I did God's work for Him, "helping Him out," maybe the pain of low self-esteem would go away.

Paula Rinehart describes this "cycle of anxiety":

When you live in the future you are always internally in motion, moving toward the next achievement, the next need to be met. . . . It's a "when I finish . . . then" approach to life where real living is put on hold. . . . As long as I was immersed in a project or moving toward a goal, life had meaning and purpose. But as soon as a blank space appeared or my schedule eased up, I was more anxious than relieved. And the only way to address the anxiety, it seemed, was to get busy again. The illusion was that some inner blessing awaited me just around the corner.[3]

8. Think about your response to the above statement, and on the scale below, evaluate your own "bent" toward perfectionism and control.

1	2	3	4	5	6	7	8	9	10

I do not relate to that statement at all!

The statement accurately depicts my life.

9. You may be wondering if you've entered the danger zone. Place an "x" in front of each of the following questions you need to answer with a yes.

❑ When situations arise that need leadership, direction, and a "voice of authority," do I find myself mentally solving the problem and then jumping in to help, even if my advice or assistance has not been requested?

❑ Do I organize family events or take charge of family crisis situations and later resent my siblings for not "doing their fair share" of the work?

❑ Do I often feel like nothing will get done if I don't take care of the situation or problem?

❑ Is it hard for me to enjoy a day off or a week's vacation? Is my mind preoccupied with the work I've left at home (or at the office), and do I feel less valuable if I'm not doing something "constructive" with my time?

❑ Do I have trouble letting people get close to me emotionally? Is it easier and less threatening to have many acquaintances, but few, if any, real "friends"?

❑ Do I focus more on the goal, product, or end result (the future) rather than on enjoying the "process" of getting there? Do I often set impossible goals and then mentally put myself down for low achievement?

❏Do I feel uncomfortable sharing my weaknesses
and needs with other people?

❏Would I rather not take on a project if my work
couldn't be as good as or better than the last
person who attempted this task? Am I uncomfortable with being "average"?

❏Do I get tired of controlling situations and
people, but feel terrified of releasing my grip?

If you answered yes to more than half of these questions,
you are not alone. We have an epidemic among Christian women who have a fear of being vulnerable, which
has catapulted into a "Tyranny of Terror." *Many women
are afraid to give up their control, fearing they will be weak,
powerless, average, open to attack, exposed, and unprotected.*

10. We know self-reliance is a form of sin. We also
know our need to control and our perfectionistic
tendencies stem from not understanding our worth
to God. Take turns reading the following verses
aloud. Summarize the truth you find.

Psalm 46:10

Jeremiah 31:3

2 Corinthians 12:9-10

1 Peter 2:9

THINK ABOUT IT
Paul was one of the most gifted leaders of all time. He was a powerful speaker, a seasoned missionary, a survivor of torture, and a man of great influence. If anyone was ever tempted to see the benefits of control, it had to be Paul. Why do you think he said, "For when I am weak, then I am strong"? What application does his statement have for your own life?

CAN CONTROLLING WOMEN EVER BREAK THE PATTERN?

As we look back at the development and defeat of fear, it helps to see ourselves "in process." My *triggering event* involved being a firstborn child with high goals, expectations, and obligations. It seemed quite natural to cover my insecurities by "control." My *reactive emotion* was panic when I realized I could never work hard enough to make everybody happy. I knew no matter how much I did, there was still more to do. My sense of *powerlessness* came when my energy ran out. My well went dry. I was exhausted!

I experienced a subliminal but growing *rage* when I realized other people were using me because I was a hard worker who always got the job done. And controlling women are good at the next step—*internal negotiating*. I convinced myself that people who are as competent as I was shouldn't be struggling like this. I rationalized: I didn't really have a problem, I had a challenge!

For a while, I chose a destructive resolution of *denial*. In time, I chose *escape* into perfectionism as my resolution for my fear of losing control.

LOOKING TO GOD

11. Pair up with another person in your group. Tell as much as you feel comfortable with about a fear you are currently experiencing. How do you feel about your significance to God right now? Have

you been a controlling woman in the past? Do you have any sin to confess? (Remember, the constructive resolution for dealing with the fear of losing control is through *sorrow, brokenness,* and *surrender,* which brings us to the place of being able to make *faith-filled decisions.*) Spend some time praying for each other. Commit to keeping what is shared confidential.

INTO OUR LIVES

Earlier in this session, we looked at the meaning of the word *vulnerable.* It seems to indicate that the person who is unprotected emotionally or physically is a vulnerable person. When we feel like victims (due to past experience or current situations) we are very open to attack, hurt, or injury.

It's easy to fall into a habit of withdrawal in order to avoid being wounded again. That's when our fear of vulnerability turns us toward control and perfectionism. However, if we're honest, we must admit that sometimes we are our own worst enemy. Our minds have a tremendous capacity for exaggeration and distortion of truth.

The flip side can be encouraging. Being vulnerable with the right people can bring deep joy, emotional "connection," and personal growth. *To be vulnerable in the positive sense is to be accessible, innocent, and exposed.* When we peel back the protective layers of our carefully crafted image and reveal ourselves to another human being who is worthy of that trust, true vulnerability brings an intimacy that breeds affection, transparency, tenderness, and understanding.

12. Read Philippians 2:19-30. How does this passage show that Paul knew how to develop open, honest, and intimate friendships? What personal application can you find for your own life? What one thing will

42

you do this week to be less controlling and more vulnerable with those closest to you?

13. Look at a few controlling women in the Bible and see if you can identify which of the ten disguises described above fit each one. In some cases, there may be more than one correct response. See Rebekah (Genesis 25:21-28, 27:1-10), Delilah (Judges 16), Jezebel (1 Kings 21:1-15), or Martha (Luke 10:38-40).

The text portions of this session were adapted from chapters 5 and 6 of *Tame Your Fears*. Read these chapters on your own for a more in-depth look at the topics discussed.

FOR MEDITATION

No one can develop freely in this world
and find a full life without feeling understood
by at least one person. . . . [She] who would see [her]self
clearly must open up to a confidant
freely chosen and worthy of such trust.[4]
Dr. Paul Tournier

Whether or not we like to admit it,
we really are all bound together by the bonds of our frailties
and cares. We just keep on fending each other off by asking
meaningless questions and giving answers back
that go with the equally meaningless ones asked us.
Sometimes I wonder how much of history has actually been
spent in conversation about the weather.[5]
Bob Benson

The quest of the woman who does too much is to live
in the humility of being who she really is.
To believe that God knew what He was doing when He made

her. And that she is—this moment—the right age,
the right gender, the right size.
She has done enough. Or more accurately,
she can never do enough to warrant the kind of love
that's been offered her in Christ.
She can only reach out and claim it.[6]

PAULA RINEHART

FOR MEMORIZATION

Come to me, all you who are weary and burdened,
and I will give you rest. Take my yoke upon you
and learn from me, for I am gentle and humble in heart,
and you will find rest for your souls.
For my yoke is easy and my burden is light.

MATTHEW 11:28-30

NOTES
1. *New Webster's Dictionary and Thesaurus of the English Language*, Bernard S. Cayne, editorial director (Danbury, CT: Lexicon Publications, Inc., 1992), page 1104.
2. Barbara Sullivan, *The Control Trap* (Minneapolis, MN: Bethany House Publishers, 1991), page 37.
3. Paula Rinehart, *Perfect Every Time* (Colorado Springs, CO: NavPress, 1992), pages 18-19.
4. Dr. Paul Tournier, as quoted in John Powell, S.J., *Why Am I Afraid to Tell You Who I Am?* (Allen, TX: Tabor Publishing, 1969), page 5.
5. Bob Benson, *See You at the House* (Nashville, TN: Generoux Nelson, 1989), page 202.
6. Rinehart, page 198.

OVERCOMING THE FEAR OF ABANDONMENT

Fear 5: Disappointing People
Fear 6: Being Rejected

WARM-UP

1. When you were growing up, who was the person you most wanted to please and *never* wanted to disappoint? Why?

2. If you were renewing a relationship with someone who once rejected you, which of the following scenarios would you prefer, and why?

   ❑ A very public gathering with many of your closest friends

   ❑ A long, quiet dinner with only the two of you

   ❑ A sporting event where the focus would be on *someone* or *something* other than your past issues with this person

WHY DO WOMEN PUT UP WITH SO MUCH?

The newspaper headline was not unusual: "San Diego Man Put On House Arrest To Await Trial." But my heart was racing.

A judge Wednesday ordered that a San Diego man charged with attempted murder of a police officer be jailed and then held under house arrest until trial. . . .

Judge Anthony J. Markham said that according to a report, Jensen "shot up everything in the house that reminded him of his wife." . . .

A standoff began at 7:45 p.m., when Jensen allegedly fired shots from a scope-equipped rifle at his wife and sheriff's deputies.

Then, as I viewed the videotape of the local news from that night, it was my sister's face that appeared on the screen of my television set. My own sister a victim of domestic violence? How could she have stayed married to an abusive man for nineteen years? What about her ten-year-old son—my nephew?!

All of us hunger for love. We spend much of our lives trying to make relationships work so we can fill the vacuum inside our souls. For most of us, no punishment could be worse than being abandoned by someone to whom we have given our love, loyalty, and commitment. Even worse, we're terrified that significant other people in our lives will know we failed at the one thing Christian women are supposed to be good at: making relationships work, especially marriage and family relationships!

Most of us would prefer to live with pain and spiritual paralysis rather than risk disappointing people who think we are models of Christian womanhood. Sometimes we choose sick marriages, plastic family reunions, and "let's pretend" church settings instead of admitting we have a problem and asking somebody for help. A few of us have functioned at this level for so long, we think it's normal.

3. If you are in a group, take turns reading through the following list of questions. As you read, put a mark in the box in front of each question that you personally feel you should answer with "yes."

❏ In one or more of your closest relationships, do you always give more than you receive?

❏ Do you fear arousing someone's anger or rage if you don't perform certain tasks to his or her liking?

❏ Do you "cover the tracks" for someone you are close to by making excuses, justifying what he (or she) hasn't done, doing work for him, or even lying to make him look better?

❏ Do you have trouble communicating in an open, honest, and appropriately confrontational manner with a certain person in your life?

❏ Do you find yourself "giving in" or "giving up" in order to keep peace in your relationship with someone?

❏ Do the emotional mood swings of another person drastically affect your planning and emotional well-being?

❏ Do you find yourself constantly "fixing things" so someone else is in a good mood or behaves in a civil manner?

4. Select one of your "yes" responses and share any frustration you have regarding this issue with the group, without naming the person involved.

UNDERSTANDING THE FEAR OF ABANDONMENT

The fear of disappointing people is rooted in the fear of abandonment. Most of us struggle with this problem at some level throughout our lifetime. A few years ago a new word started cropping up in informal conversations everywhere: *codependency*. This word plays a vital role

47

in the lives of all of us who are afraid of disappointing people.

In her book *From Bondage to Bonding*, Nancy Groom defines codependency as,

> A self-focused way of life in which a person blind to his or her true self continually reacts to others—being controlled by and seeking to control their behavior, attitudes, and/or opinions, resulting in spiritual sterility, loss of authenticity, and absence of intimacy.[1]

At one time or another, *all* of us have dealt with some level of codependency. Every time we feel controlled by other people, we choose a course of action.

Codependents feel controlled by someone else all the time. But the important key is that codependents live in a constant state of denial about how they are actually relating to the controlling partner in a relationship.

Groom says,

> Think of a relationship continuum with healthy mutual interdependence at one end and debilitating codependency at the other. We all fall somewhere in between. . . . [But] the longer a person pursues codependent strategies for dealing with life, the more codependent he or she becomes. Eventually those strategies become an addictive way of life—a person's primary and compulsive method for relating to self and others.[2]

> Mutual interdependence occurs when two persons, secure in God's acceptance, mutually give and receive love and forgiveness, without demanding approval or conformity to expectations in return, resulting in spiritual vitality, a balanced view of self, and genuine intimacy.[3]

5. On the scale that follows, indicate where you think you are in your most "challenging" personal relationship at this time in your life.

1	2	3	4	5	6	7	8	9	10
Debilitating							Healthy Mutual		
Codependence							Interdependence		

6. Have you ever had the kind of interdependent relationship Groom describes? If so, what were the personal benefits you received?

HOW DID MY SISTER CHOOSE CODEPENDENCY AS A LIFESTYLE?

Why did my sister keep her mental and sexual abuse such a secret? Why did she enable her husband to continue in his destructive path by making calls to appease his creditors? Why did she always make excuses for him when family members visited? Why did she justify his childish behavior to their son? When he became raging mad and destroyed expensive personal property, why did she let him "get back in her good graces" the next day as he repeatedly came with his familiar "I'm sorry"?

Triggering situation: Prior to Megan's whirlwind romance with Michael Jensen, she had been in love with a man her father disapproved of. With a deep desire to meet the expectations of her family and to protect her father's ministry from potential controversy, she broke off the relationship, even though the decision brought her deep personal pain.

She married Michael within a year after saying good-bye to her first love. Michael was the fifth child born to an economically deprived family, and he was the only child in the family released for adoption. Although he was raised by parents who adored him and gave him every benefit money and love could provide, he knew he was the only child abandoned by his birth parents. Thus, his "love tank" was always on "empty" and the only way he knew how to compensate was to totally control Megan with an unhealthy, obsessive love.

49

Reactive emotion: Megan began to experience fear on many levels. Michael began destroying property when he was angry. At times she feared for her own safety and that of her son. On another level, she was deeply afraid of hurting the testimony of her mother and father if word of Michael's violence and their marriage problems became known. She had recurring fears that *she* might be the person causing Michael's problems. Perhaps if she was a more submissive wife, he wouldn't become so violent. She felt alone, and the fear was overpowering.

7. When we face the fear of disappointing people or the fear of rejection, we often feel lonely. How does loneliness feel?

Powerlessness: It didn't take long for Megan to feel powerless and betrayed. Earlier, her conservative Christian father had kept her from marrying the man she had cared for so deeply. Later, Michael eroded her confidence and made her feel incapable of changing her downward spiral. Finally, she felt betrayed by God.

Rage: After a while, anger began to fester. And then Megan's emotions turned to rage. She had tried her best to be an obedient daughter and a submissive wife. Did God see what was happening and how miserable she was?

8. Was there ever a time in your life when you felt betrayed by God? If so, did this feeling of rejection lead you to a dead-end resolution involving self-reliance, or to sorrow, brokenness, and surrender?

Internal negotiating: At times like this, most of us struggle deeply. During the powerless stage, we tend to get our focus off Christ and on our own crisis and need. After rage sets in, we decide *to do something ourselves* since the people we trusted haven't come through for us. Thus, self-reliance becomes our crutch. Our internal negotiation always leads us to take action.

Destructive resolution: We often wind up choosing denial, defeat, bitterness, or escape into obsessive/compulsive behaviors. In the beginning, Megan chose *denial*. She had married this man and she was going to make it work. She began convincing herself his emotional fits of rage were like any man venting his disapproval. His sexual obsession and outlandish physical demands were sometimes unbearable, but God said she was supposed to give herself to her husband and she did.

In the end Megan chose survival through an *escape* called codependence. She wasn't happy, but at least she could try to "manage" this difficult situation. She became skilled at hiding Michael's mistakes, covering up the aftermath of his violence, and making excuses for his behavior. For years, it seemed like the right decision. It made her feel like a "biblically correct" wife; it kept her from embarrassing her parents with a divorced daughter; it kept a raging husband under control most of the time. But her life was spiritually sterile. She lost self-respect and intimacy.

9. The circumstances may have been very different, but have you ever felt as spiritually sterile as Megan felt? If so, how did you try to fix your problem?

10. How do we wind up with this problem? Take turns reading the following descriptions, and place a check mark in front of the one you identify with most.

❑ *Fear of disappointing God.* Most of us have been raised with a strong work ethic and we believe in the concept of "serving people in love." We believe giving of ourselves to help others is basic to what Scripture teaches. With our deep desire to have a strong Christian home, we wind up enabling our "less spiritual" spouses or family members to look more godly by controlling their behavior, attitudes, and opinions.

❑ *Filling the donut hole.* Once, as I twirled a sumptuous glazed Krispy Kreme on my finger before attacking it with the first crushing bite, I realized my "real self" was a lot like the hole in the middle—empty, lost, and abandoned, but never declared missing because it was never noticed. No matter how hard we have tried to please other people and God by doing more for Him or them, it hasn't brought contentment. So we move into looking for fulfillment by managing another person, but the "hole in our soul" is still there.

❑ *Lost childhood.* Women who have been abused or rejected as children easily fall into codependent relationships in their adulthood. They often experience an undercurrent of guilt, believing they could have changed the situation or stopped the abuse or rejection of the past if they were smart enough or strong enough. This leads to low self-esteem, which reinforces a cycle of trying to be helpful or good enough to please the people around them.

❑ *Misunderstanding submission.* Christian women know the Bible teaches that the husband is the head of the house, as Christ is the head of the church. The guidelines for a successful and happy marriage are definitely found in Scripture. However, some verses have been lifted from their context to authenticate an incorrect teaching about Christian marriage.

Often, the woman who has been taught that her chief duty is "to please her man" believes that she should just put up with mental, physical, and sexual abuse. This woman often hears her husband say, "If you would just submit to me the way the Bible teaches, I wouldn't have to yell at you (or discipline you)." The codependent woman believes that *she* is responsible for his negative actions and attitude. Her self-esteem is so fragile, she quickly accepts the blame for almost anything!

In 1 Corinthians 7:4 [we] accept Paul's teaching that the husband rules over the wife's body—ignoring the rest of that verse . . . that says the wife rules over the husband's body. In that same chapter, verse 10, Paul declares that a wife should not separate from her husband. Yet, how few women are counseled in the rest of that same verse—*"but if she does"* . . . Paul left the door open for extreme cases.

The wife is called upon to be subject to her man (Ephesians 5:22), but hardly anyone notices that in 5:21 Paul has used exactly the same word to call every Christian into similar submission to every other. . . . The abusive husband quotes Hebrews 12:7, which extols God's disciplining of His faithful, and twists it to suggest that the man ought to keep his mature adult wife in line in the same way one might discipline a small child, or God might discipline an errant saint.[4]

11. What do you think about this understanding of biblical submission?

We have emphasized the need to develop a biblical, constructive resolution for fear. Consider the four steps involved in a constructive choice to resolve the fear of being rejected or abandoned.

12. *Sorrow.* When we stop trying to fix our problems and allow the sorrow of a fallen world to penetrate us, we grieve deeply. Read Job 19:17-20 and summarize the thoughts Job expressed during the time he felt abandoned.

13. *Brokenness.* When we come to the place of being humble enough to say, "Lord, I need You," we bring a humble heart to God. Instead of continuing in our self-reliant mode, we seek God-dependence. Read Psalm 51:1-5. What sin(s) have you committed to avoid abandonment?

14. *Surrender.* Surrender is an act of giving up my plan and accepting His plan. Read Psalm 51:10-12. How did David show he was surrendering?

15. *Faith-filled decision.* Trust is exchanged for fear when we have finally let go of the situation, the person, the deep emotion of fear, the codependent relationship, or the past abandonment issues. At this point we can make the faith-filled decision to believe Hebrews 13:5-6 (NKJV):

For He Himself has said, "I will never leave you nor forsake you." So we may boldly say, "The Lord is my helper, I will not fear. What can man do to me?"

What does that verse mean to you?

LOOKING TO GOD

If you are meeting in a group, your leader may ask the large group to divide into pairs to share your answers to the following questions.

16. Do you have any codependent relationships in your life right now? If so, what do you think God wants you to do as a first step?

17. How can someone pray for you?

Spend a few minutes praying for the specific requests that were mentioned.

INTO OUR LIVES

18. a. Think of one of your major fears. Trace your experience and resulting resolution by writing a brief description about each of the following steps in the chain reaction. (It might be helpful to reread the example on pages 11-15.)

▼ Triggering event/person/situation
▼ Reactive emotion

▼ Sense of powerlessness
▼ Rage
▼ Internal negotiating

b. At this point, did you choose a *constructive* or a *destructive* resolution for the fear? Describe your destructive choice of denial, defeat, bitterness, or escape or share your constructive course of action, which usually begins with sorrow and brokenness, then surrender, and finally a faith-filled decision.
   Keep in mind that when we practice the constructive resolution, the steps go quickly and it is sometimes hard to define the exact point at which brokenness turns to surrender.

19. Read the intriguing story about Elijah recorded in 1 Kings 17. At what point in this chapter do you think Elijah felt abandoned? At what time in your life has your "brook dried up"? When you are abandoned—without the support of friends, family, or helpful resources—where do you turn?

20. Max Lucado says, "When all of earth turns against you all of heaven turns toward you. To keep your balance in a crooked world, look at the mountains. Think of home."[5] Take a few minutes to list five things you can do today that will give you a "heavenly perspective" in the middle of your current life situation.

The text portions of this session were adapted from chapters 7 and 8 of *Tame Your Fears*. You can read these chapters on your own to learn more about the topics discussed.

FOR MEDITATION

When we face how deeply disappointed we are with our
relationships, it then becomes possible to recognize
the ugliness of what before seemed reasonable.
When I realize how badly I want someone
to come through for me in a way no one has,
then (and not until then) can I see how hard I work
either to get what I want or to protect myself
from the anguish of more disappointment.[6]

Dr. Larry Crabb

Few things make us more aware of our need for the Lord
than rejection. The only final cure
for the frowning face of rejection is His smiling face of love
and acceptance. And the more we wait for Him,
the less we'll wait in fear of future rejection.[7]

Dr. Lloyd Ogilvie

Here and there we stumble blind in grief
through our Gethsemanes and find the ground already
stained with His blood. In our Gethsemanes there's an unseen
plaque on every twisted tree, "Jesus was here."
He is still here, and we can bear with our Good Fridays
if we let our Thursdays call to mind the glorious solitude
of Him who conquered loneliness.[8]

Calvin Miller

FOR MEMORIZATION

For He Himself has said,
"I will never leave you nor forsake you."
So we may boldly say, "The Lord is my helper,
I will not fear. What can man do to me?"
Hebrews 13:5-6 (NKJV)

NOTES

1. Nancy Groom, *From Bondage to Bonding* (Colorado Springs, CO: NavPress, 1991), page 21.
2. Groom, page 21.

3. Groom, page 156.
4. Robert Hemfelt, Frank Minirth, and Paul Meier, *Love Is a Choice* (Nashville, TN: Thomas Nelson Publishers, 1989), pages 98-99.
5. Max Lucado, *And the Angels Were Silent* (Portland, OR: Multnomah, 1992), page 163.
6. Larry Crabb, *Inside Out* (Colorado Springs, CO: NavPress, 1988), page 176.
7. Lloyd Ogilvie, *12 Steps to Living Without Fear* (Waco, TX: Word Books, 1987), page 128.
8. Calvin Miller, "Alone," *Moody* (Chicago, IL: Moody Bible Institute, March 1991), page 23.

OVERCOMING THE FEAR OF TRUTH
Fear 7: Facing My Past
Fear 8: Losing My Faith

WARM-UP

1. When you have time to reflect, which of the following things are you the most likely to think about? Explain.

   ▼ Your mistakes of the past
   ▼ Your goals for the future

2. If you had serious doubts about your faith, who would you talk to? Why?

THE FEAR OF FACING THE PAST

3. On your own, read through the following list of ten "If onlys," and place a check in front of each one you can relate to.

❑ "If only I could live that one day over . . ."

❑ "If only I had come to Christ sooner . . ."

❑ "If only I hadn't married the first man who showed an interest in me . . ."

❑ "If only I had taken the other route home . . ."

❑ "If only I could take back those words of criticism . . ."

❑ "If only I hadn't taken up that bad habit . . ."

❑ "If only I had left that miserable job sooner . . ."

❑ "If only I had resisted the flirtations of that man . . ."

❑ "If only I had spent more time with my children . . ."

❑ "If only I had the courage to confront my father/mother/brother/grandfather about what (s)he did to me . . ."

❑ "If only I hadn't waited so long to have children . . ."

Some of the memories Christian women shudder to face include a parent's abandonment, sexual abuse, a church that took advantage of an eager worker, being treated as inferior, an abortion, losing a man to another woman, being passed over for promotion, an affair, mistakes as a mother—the list is endless.

4. As you look back on the "yesterdays" of your life, do you have any regret or painful memory that has been a hindrance to you? If you feel comfortable talking about it, share your thoughts with the group.

5. Have you ever felt afraid to face your past? Explain.

Many of us have been held in the grip of our fearful memories for too many years. Some of us spend a lifetime trying to work hard enough and smile long enough to convince ourselves and other people that we're okay. But we're always looking over our shoulder, running from the truth.

6. Evaluate the way you currently feel about your past.

1   2   3   4   5   6   7   8   9   10
I am often consumed   I have resolved
with fears regarding   my fears concerning
past issues.   past issues.

Sometimes we believe that if we give ourselves time to face our past, we will be overwhelmed by shame, guilt, and more anger. So rather than exploring the feelings those memories reveal, it's easier to bury our fears in denial, defeat, bitterness, or escapes—and the cycle of fear continues. But God has a different plan.

7. Read through the following Scriptures and make any comment on God's instruction for dealing with the wrong choices of yesterday or His response to past issues.

Psalm 103:3-4

Psalm 103:10-12

1 Peter 5:6-7

1 John 1:9

Throughout this study we have been outlining the chain reaction involved in choosing a constructive or a destructive resolution for fear. Take a moment to identify one of your worst fears involving the past. It might involve a mistake, a wrong choice, a regret, or false shame you still carry for victimization. (You may or may not have worked through the fear yet.)

If you feel comfortable sharing your responses with the group in this section, write out your response to each word in the chain reaction and volunteer comments accordingly. (In this section, some people will have very personal fears to work through and it is absolutely fine to be a listener, rather than a participant.)

8. Describe the triggering event or situation.

9. What was your reactive emotion (such as shock, hurt, anger, shame, terror)?

10. How did this situation make you feel powerless?

11. When you are full of rage over past issues, are you more inclined to keep it inside or do you talk about it?

12. When it comes to the fear of facing your past, are you more angry with *yourself* (reasoning that if you had been smarter or stronger, you could have stopped the person or event triggering your fear) or are you more angry at *the person who caused your pain* (realizing he or she was selfish and hurtful)?

When we get angry because fear has stripped us of our power, we want to be self-reliant because relying on other people or on God hasn't seemed to help. As our anger cools slightly, we begin our "fix-it" program. We are sick of being controlled by fear, and something has to change or we will break down emotionally.

At this crucial point, we allow our "internal churning" to steer us toward a constructive or destructive course of action. Questions surface that have no answers, such as, "Why did I take that position in the first place?" "Why didn't I set an earlier curfew for my daughter?" "Why did I give in to peer pressure?"

13. Write out the haunting question that sometimes still surfaces as you think about your fear regarding a past issue.

When we get no answers to those questions, we often seek a destructive course of action for dealing with the fears that resurface. We can sometimes convince ourselves to *deny* there was ever a problem in the first place. More often, we feel *defeated* by the fears from the past that haunt us today and tell ourselves the future will be another version of a terrible past.

Sometimes we begin to blame all the negatives in our lives on the events, people, and situations that caused us to fear in the first place. At this point *bitterness* takes over. At times we feel driven to seek revenge. More often, the end result is an *escape* into obsessive/addictive patterns.

14. If you chose a destructive resolution for your fear and feel comfortable talking about what happened, share your response with the group.

15. If you chose a constructive resolution involving *sorrow* (grief for the injustices in your life or sadness for your wrong choices), share how that led to *brokenness* (humility before God), and into *surrender* (God-reliance instead of self-reliance), and then on to the ability to begin making *faith-filled decisions*.

Much of our ability to face the past in order to get on with the future is wrapped up in the power of forgiveness. Surrender to God always brings us to the point of being able to make the faith-filled decision to forgive.

Booker T. Washington once said, "I will not permit any man to narrow and degrade my soul by making me hate him."[1] I think Washington was really saying that when our days are consumed with thoughts of revenge, past abuses, or why we hate ourselves for the wrong choices we have made, we are chaining ourselves to a prison of our own making.

16. Do you find it difficult or easy to forgive those who've wronged you and to forgive yourself for past mistakes? Explain.

17. Read Matthew 18:21-22. What do you think Jesus was trying to teach Peter about forgiveness in this passage?

THE FEAR OF FACING OUR DOUBTS ABOUT GOD

Another major fear of the truth involves our inability to admit our occasional doubts about Christianity. Perhaps the most haunting thought a Christian woman can ever have is this: "What if the God I have always believed in, the faith I have affirmed to others, and the beliefs I have taught my children are inaccurate? And why *does* God allow good people to suffer?"

18. a. John 10:10 (KJV) says, "I am come that they might have life, and that they might have it more abundantly." What expectations did you have when you signed on to become a Christian?

b. Has your Christian experience been the same or different from what you expected? Explain.

Sometimes, in the middle of our spiritual journey, an event or crisis brings a cloud of doubt over our faith. Christians who are struggling with doubts almost never talk about it. They are too ashamed. People might think they are heretics. Undiscussed, the doubts increase and the fear magnifies.

Josh McDowell said,

> For every confirmed skeptic I encounter, I meet at least a dozen sincere believers who struggle with doubt. At times their apprehension is casual, but at other times it is grave. These people want to believe God, but for whatever reason, wrestle with thoughts and feelings to the contrary. And, unfortunately, when doubt enters the believer's experience, it threatens to paralyze him.[2]

19. Since you became a Christian, have you ever had serious doubts about the reality of God, the Bible, and/or His Word? If so, did you tell anybody about the struggle you were having, or was it too embarrassing to bring up?

Philip Yancey once said, "Fear, not doubt, is faith's opposite." In other words, if we are willing to look into the face of doubt, seeking truth (not fearing it), we will find a renewed faith. When we shrink back, unwilling to face legitimate doubt about the truth of God's Word, the justice of God's plan, and the disappointments in our lives, we live in a fearful cage of growing disillusionment.

20. Do you agree or disagree with the following statement?

    Doubts about God should not lead to denial, defeat, bitterness, or escape. They should lead to a "truth-search." Asking questions related to our doubts will lead to a strengthened faith as we discover truth in the process.

21. What advice do you have for the person in this group who might be struggling with doubts about her faith right now?

LOOKING TO GOD

Your leader may ask the large group to divide into groups of two or three to share your answers to some of the following questions.

22. Since this study began, have you had any specific victory over fear in your life? If so, describe it.

23. Do you believe you have dealt with the fears of your past—the mistakes, regrets, wrong choices, or victimization—or are you still living in fear?

24. Are you struggling with any doubts about your faith right now?

25. How can someone pray for you?

Spend a few minutes praying for the specific praises and requests that were mentioned.

INTO OUR LIVES

26. Several Bible characters had serious regrets to deal with because of the wrong choices of their lives. See Eve (Genesis 3:1-7), Abram and Sarai (Genesis 16), David (2 Samuel 11–12), or Peter (John 18:15-17,25-27).

27. Sometime this week, contact a friend or acquaintance who might be struggling over past issues or doubts about her faith. Make an appointment to have an informal time to talk (preferably over coffee, tea, or lunch). Let her know you've been praying for her and would love to be a "sounding board" for her questions or spiritual concerns. (Make a conscious effort to listen more than you talk.)

The text portions of this session were adapted from chapters 9 and 10 of *Tame Your Fears*. Read these chapters on your own for a more in-depth look at the topics discussed.

FOR MEDITATION

You have been damaged. But you have great hope.
The mercy of God does not eradicate the damage, at least not
in this life, but it soothes the soul and draws
it forward to a hope that purifies and sets free.

*Allow the pain of the past and the travail of the change
process to create fresh new life in you
and to serve as a bridge over which another victim
may walk from death to life.*[3]

DAN ALLENDER

*Forgive, and you can heal, move on, reduce your health risks,
lighten your spirit. . . . Forgive, and you free all the energy
you are currently using in reviewing old injuries,
fantasizing revenge, craving justice.
Forgive, and the piece of you that was tied up with rage
is free to be much, much more.*[4]

JUDITH SILLS

*When our faith in God transcends our doubts about God . . .
we will not find ready-made answers to all of life's questions.
And we will not find solutions
to all of life's problems or acquire protection
against all of life's tragedies. We will, however,
find a framework for life that brings purpose to our days,
meaning to our hearts, and solace to our hurts.*[5]

GARY E. PARKER

FOR MEMORIZATION

**He does not treat us as our sins deserve
or repay us according to our iniquities.
For as high as the heavens are above the earth,
so great is his love for those who fear him;
as far as the east is from the west,
so far has He removed our transgressions from us.**

PSALM 103:10-12

NOTES
1. Booker T. Washington, quoted in *Great Quotes & Illustrations*, compiled by George Sweeting (Waco, TX: Word Books, 1985), page 119.
2. Josh McDowell, quoted in the foreword of *Doubt, A Road to Growth*, by Jackie Hudson (San Bernardino, CA: Here's Life Publishers, Inc., 1987), page 9.
3. Dan B. Allender, *The Wounded Heart* (Colorado Springs, CO: NavPress, 1990), page 247.

69

4. Judith Sills, Ph.D., *Excess Baggage* (New York: Viking Penguin, 1993), pages 229-230.
5. Gary E. Parker, *The Gift of Doubt: From Crisis to Authentic Faith* (San Francisco, CA: Harper and Row, 1990), page 18.

Overcoming the Fear of Making Wrong Choices

Fear 9: Getting Trapped
Fear 10: Achieving Success/Admitting Failure

WARM-UP

1. A cartoonist depicted a woman at a fork in the road who crashed into a pole between the two choices. As she stumbled out of her car with broken bones and open wounds, she said, "I just couldn't decide which way to go." Can you identify with this woman? Do you often find yourself paralyzed by indecision, or is it easy for you to make decisive choices?

2. In what one area of your life are you the most afraid of failing?

SEARCHING FOR THE "DOT"

As early as I can remember, I always wanted to make a difference in the lives of other people. I desired to be a woman of vision, passion, and commitment. I embarked on a quest to find the "dot" in the center of God's will for my life. I had often been instructed to seek God's "perfect" plan for my life. Being totally convinced there was an ideal blueprint was comforting. It meant if I could just find the right niche, hard choices would no longer plague me.

Finding God's "dot" would eliminate the gripping fear of choosing a path of "second best." I dreaded choosing incorrectly and finding out years later that I should have followed a different path in order to please God more fully.

3. Mark the box beside each of the following statements that you believe to be true.

❑ I believe God has a perfect blueprint for every Christian's life.

❑ I believe God gives Christians the right to choose regarding many life-altering options while still being in His will.

❑ I can be 100 percent sure of God's individual will for my life.

❑ I believe if a woman doesn't marry God's ideal man for her life, she will totally ruin the lives of the man she was supposed to marry and of the woman her husband was supposed to marry.

4. Read the following Scripture passages and summarize the truth you find.

Psalm 19:7-8

Psalm 32:8

Proverbs 3:5-6

Micah 6:8

5. Do you think these verses teach that there is a specific, inflexible blueprint for the believer, or that God's will might involve wider choices, within His guidelines, for a successful and meaningful Christian life?

6. Some of the fears that came from my dot-in-the-center-of-God's-will theology may be similar to fears you had in earlier years. Place a mark in front of each fear that is similar to one you have experienced. Share your responses.

☐ If I attend the wrong college, I will meet people who could negatively influence my life.

☐ If I marry the wrong man, I will ruin both our lives and the lives of our future children and grandchildren.

☐ If I don't major in the right field, I could wind up in a job that is unfulfilling, beneath my potential, and out of God's will.

☐ If I don't go into full-time Christian service, I may fall short of God's plan for my life.

❏ If I don't choose to live in the right neighborhood, I may lose out on meeting a neighbor God wanted me to win to the Lord.

7. What possible dangers could come out of this type of thinking?

THINK ABOUT IT
Haddon Robinson says,

If we ask, "How can I know the will of God?" we may be asking the wrong question. The Scriptures do not command us to find God's will for most of life's choices, nor do we have any passage instructing us on how it can be determined . . . the Christian community has never agreed on how God provides us with such special revelation. Yet we persist in searching for God's will because decisions require thought and sap energy. We seek relief from the responsibility of decision-making and we feel less threatened by being passive rather than active when making important choices.[1]

▼ Do you think it is right or wrong to ask God for "neon signs" and specific, well-defined direction for our lives? Why?
▼ Are you comfortable with basing your major choices on your knowledge of God's character and His Word, and then, after praying and seeking wise counsel from godly people, going ahead with a decision? Why, or why not?

The fear of getting trapped in a dead-end life situation makes many women wonder how their lives would have turned out differently had they taken a different fork in the road.

8. Place a mark in front of any of these fears of getting trapped that you have identified with at some point in your life.

❑ "If I can't get away from the ugliness of my past, I will be destined for failure."

❑ "If I take this job now because of economic necessity, I may close the door on a better opportunity for career advancement in a position more suited to my background and education."

❑ "If I don't work harder and outdo the competition in my office, I may not get a promotion."

❑ "If I'm promoted, I may feel pressured to 'succeed' at a level that will compromise balance in other important areas of my life."

❑ "If I say no to personal or professional opportunities in order to stay physically and emotionally healthy now, I may never have other opportunities when I'm ready for them."

❑ "If I choose to marry, I may get a man as dysfunctional as my father, and I will never let that happen!"

❑ "If I don't marry this man, someone I'm more compatible with might not come along, and I'd be sorry I turned him down."

❑ "If I do marry this man—even though we seem perfectly suited for one another—I may discover later I have shut myself out from reaching my highest potential in my work or ministry because of the encumbrances of family responsibilities."

❑ "If I leave a relationship that is destroying me, I will never have a better relationship."

❑ "If I have a baby now, I may interrupt my career and never recapture the momentum and job success I've worked so hard to obtain."

❑ "If I wait to have a child until I'm older and more established in my marriage and in my career, I may increase my risk of having a baby with mental or physical disabilities."

❑ "If I don't pursue infertility treatment, I will never know complete fulfillment as a mother and eventually as a grandmother."

9. Which of the above scenarios has brought you the greatest fear of getting trapped? Why?

In the middle of our lives, from about ages thirty-five to forty-five, our marriages and careers have generally settled into a routine. This is a time when many women question their life choices and ask, *Is that all there is?*[2]

10. Have you ever asked yourself, "Is that all there is?" What were the circumstances in your life at the time?

THE PARADOX: FEARING SUCCESS AND FAILURE

Some people would say I've had a lot of successes: a growing ministry, a few books published, a couple of appearances on national television, a few articles in Christian periodicals—but sometimes I have this haunting feeling that I might have picked the wrong definition of success. My mind goes back to an incident I first shared in *Speak Up With Confidence*:

> I had jumped out of bed early, showered, dressed hurriedly, and sat reading the paper at the kitchen table while enjoying a freshly brewed cup of coffee.
> J.P. (Jason Paul) came downstairs a few minutes later. I made him some breakfast and returned to my coffee. Minutes later while peering at me over his cereal bowl, he said, "Mama, you look so pretty today."
> I couldn't believe it. On most days I'm quite dressed up—always a bit more comfortable in a suit and heels than in a pair of blue jeans and sneakers. On the day in question, I had dressed for leisure—nothing special, just slacks and a sweater.
> We made eye contact, and I questioned him: "Honey, why do you think I look pretty today? These are old clothes, and usually Mother's wearing something nicer."
> He flashed his gorgeous blue eyes and smiled at me. "It's because," he said thoughtfully, "when you're all dressed up, I know you're going out some place, but when you look like this, I know you're all mine!"
> His answer was like an arrow, piercing my heart and pinning me to the back of the chair. It had never dawned on me that this little boy could tell if I had *time* for him by what I was wearing on any given day.[3]

I faced the fear of becoming a failure at the one thing I most wanted to succeed at—motherhood. I was allowing my success in ministry potentially to drive me to fail at one of my main tasks on this earth: being a great mom to Jason Kent. New choices were necessary, but in the middle of my fear of failure, I did not know how to begin making faith-filled decisions that would redirect my priorities. I bottomed out!

11. Erwin Lutzer once said, "Many who are climbing the ladder of success have their ladders leaning against the wrong walls." Name one or two of the "wrong walls" your ladder of success might be leaning against.

My undefined priorities made me fear failing at home. Consider the chain reaction my fear followed:

Triggering event: My ministry was demanding more days away from home and more preoccupation at home while I answered mail and returned phone calls. I had never decided what was most important to me, so I let aggressive meeting planners, urgent mail, and ministry preparation keep me so busy I never thought about saying no.

12. What is the danger of undefined priorities?

Reactive emotion: I began fearing success and failure at the same time. The more successful I was in ministry, the more time demands were in my life. I didn't know how to set limits. I was afraid of failure, because in my mind, if I hurt my child by being too busy, no other form of success could make up for that type of failure.

Rage: When I lived through overcommitment, I was furious with myself. I would return home from the airport after three days on the road, tiptoe into my son's bedroom, pray over his sleeping figure—and realize I had just missed three days of his life. I hated myself! When I saw my husband reading a book or playing a game with Jason, a surge of anger would envelop me. I wanted the same privilege and freedom—but my schedule was so full I rarely had time for such luxuries.

13. Do you get angry when you are overcommitted? If so, at whom or what is your anger directed?

Internal negotiating: At different times, I tried all four ways of resolving my fear of failing as a mom: denial, defeat, bitterness, and escape.

14. I convinced myself that I always spent "quality time" with my son, and that's what mattered, not the quantity. I did not have a problem! Do you ever find yourself rationalizing your way into denial about overcommitment or failure? Explain.

15. I was constantly exhausted and felt like giving up. Have you ever been in that state? Explain.

16. There was one year when I blamed my husband (because if he made more money, I could slow down), the Little League committee (for scheduling my son's games when I couldn't attend), and God

(for not caring enough to supply me with the joy I had lost). Who or what have you blamed for your problems while you have struggled with the fear of failure?

17. I found myself sinking into the compulsive addictions of work and perfectionism. What escapes, if any, are you using right now to numb the fear of failure in your life?

Over time, I have learned how to arrive at a constructive resolution more quickly. I've also learned how miserable I am when I go back into my I'll-take-care-of-the-problem-myself mode. It just doesn't work!

When I experienced *sorrow*, I grieved for the time I had lost with my child because of overcommitment. I felt deep sadness for the times I yelled at him because of my own fatigue. I wept for the false guilt I had placed on my husband, and I lamented over my inability to relax. This led to *brokenness*, a humility before God. I prayed, "Lord, I'm hurting. I'm a failure as a wife and a mother. I'm a phony Christian leader and I'm at the end of my resources. None of my successes mean anything because they have not brought happiness. I cannot go on like this." For me, *surrender* meant getting on my knees with my precious date book in my hand and offering it to God.

18. What is the most tangible thing you could offer to God right now that would represent your surrender to Him?

Out of the yielding pattern of sorrow, brokenness, and surrender comes an empowerment that sets former fears free. Instead of being in bondage to indecision, we have a supernatural strength to make faith-filled decisions.

LOOKING TO GOD

19. What has God been speaking to your heart about during the six sessions of this study?

20. What part of the constructive resolution for dealing with fear is the greatest challenge for you? Explain.

❑ *Sorrow*: Allowing yourself to grieve over fear brought on by a fallen world.

❑ *Brokenness*: Experiencing true humility before God with your focus off the fear and on Him.

❑ *Surrender*: Giving up your self-reliance by a specific act of "heart submission" and choosing God-dependence.

❑ *Faith-filled decisions*: The ability to choose faith over fear in real-life situations.

21. How can the group pray for you specifically?

Spend some time in prayer together. End your prayer time by reading the following prayer together.

Lord, as I go on from this point in my life, give me the grace to realize life on this earth will never be completely free from anxiety. I know the enemy will harass me with memories of failure from the past, and I will be tempted to fall back into old patterns of handling my fears.

Protect me from the bondage of denial and defeat. Guard my heart from the cancer of bitterness. Keep me from my favorite escapes.

Lord, when fear surfaces, help me to grieve over the pain without shame and let my broken heart turn me to humble surrender and forgiveness. Enable me to practice making faith-filled decisions as I submit to Your authority in my life. Keep me from demanding instant answers, and help me to understand the simple truth: Faith that begins with fear will end up closer to You.

INTO OUR LIVES

22. Dealing with lifelong fears is a dynamic process of choosing to face the fear, acknowledging the pain, and implementing a constructive resolution. The Bible is our source of truth. Look back at each of the previous five sessions in this study and list Scripture verses or ideas that emphasize an important truth you learned.

▼ Overcoming the Fear of Things That Haven't Happened . . . Yet!
▼ Overcoming the Fear of Being Vulnerable
▼ Overcoming the Fear of Abandonment
▼ Overcoming the Fear of Truth
▼ Overcoming the Fear of Making Wrong Choices

The text portions of this session were adapted from chapters 11 and 12 of *Tame Your Fears*. You can read these chapters on your own to learn more about the topics discussed.

FOR MEDITATION

God took humankind very seriously
when He gave us the gift of choice;
perhaps more seriously than we take ourselves.
We frequently and almost carelessly . . . abdicate
our autonomy and let the community,
the government, or the church decide for us.[4]
MARY LOU CUMMINGS

You have failed in the past.
You are failing now in some way.
You will fail in the future.
You weren't perfect in the past.
You won't be perfect in the future.
Your children will not be perfect, either.
When you fail, allow yourself to feel disappointment,
but not disapproval. . . . You can fail
and not be a failure![5]
H. NORMAN WRIGHT

Biographies of bold disciples begin with chapters
of honest terror. Fear of death.
Fear of failure. Fear of loneliness.
Fear of a wasted life. . . . Faith begins when you see God
on the mountain and you are in the valley
and you know that you're too weak to make the climb.
You see what you need . . . you see what you have . . .
and it isn't enough . . . but He is! . . .
Faith that begins with fear will end up nearer the Father.[6]
MAX LUCADO

FOR MEMORIZATION

So do not fear, for I am with you;
do not be dismayed, for I am your God.

I will strengthen you and help you;
I will uphold you with my righteous right hand.
ISAIAH 41:10

NOTES

1. Haddon W. Robinson, quoted from the foreword in *Decision Making and the Will of God*, by Garry Friesen (Portland, OR: Multnomah Press, 1980), book jacket.
2. Jean Lush, *Emotional Phases of a Woman's Life* (Old Tappan, NJ: Fleming H. Revell Co., 1987), page 109.
3. Carol Kent, *Speak Up With Confidence* (Nashville, TN: Thomas Nelson Publishers, 1987), page 172.
4. Mary Lou Cummings, quoted in *Inspiring Quotations*, compiled by Albert M. Wells, Jr. (Nashville, TN: Thomas Nelson Publishers, 1988), page 56.
5. H. Norman Wright, quoted in an article by Judy Anderson, "Learning Unconditional Love," *Moody* (Chicago, IL: Moody Bible Institute, February 1993), page 53.
6. Max Lucado, *In the Eye of the Storm* (Dallas, TX: Word Publishing, 1991), pages 200-201.

HELP FOR LEADERS

There are several ways this study can be used effectively. *Small group Bible study.* This guide is intended to be used in a group of four to twelve women. Because God has designed Christians to function as a body, we learn and grow more when we interact with others than we would on our own. If you are thinking of doing this study of your own, prayerfully consider who you could recruit to join you in working through this study. If you have a group of more than twelve, we suggest that you divide into groups of six or so. With more than twelve people, you begin to move into a large group dynamic, and not everyone has an opportunity (or the courage) to participate.

Large group Bible study. Many churches have women's programs that include a weekly Bible study. This study guide could be done very effectively if the main teacher prepares lectures on the topics covered in each session. The weekly Bible study could begin with a joint assembly of all participants in the main meeting area for a brief time of singing, followed by a message given by the main teacher on the topic of the week. Then the women would divide into smaller groups of six to ten people, with someone assigned to facilitate leading each group. Since the study guide sessions are geared to ninety minutes each, you will not be able to discuss all the questions in each section. (The entire Bible study with the main lecture, movement to small groups, and discussion time should not be longer than two hours.) If you wish to discuss more, you can plan twelve weeks for the study, allowing two weeks for each of the six sessions.

Women's Sunday school class. If your church has an all female Sunday morning class, you would be able to use the study guide for one of the quarters during the year. The material is applicable for married and single women. Since most Sunday school quarters are geared to twelve weeks, the teacher could lecture on the first topic during the first week of the quarter, followed by discussion from the study guide on the second week, and so on. Another option would be to take two weeks to mix lecture and discussion for each of the six sessions. Many Sunday school classes are only forty-five minutes long, while the study guide sessions are set up for ninety minutes of interaction and discussion. If the teacher would prefer more lecture time, simply disregard some of the discussion questions.

THE FIRST SESSION

You or someone else in the group should open the meeting with a short prayer dedicating your time together to the Lord.

At some point during the session, go over the following guidelines. They can make a discussion more fruitful, especially when you are dealing with issues that truly matter to people.

▼ *Confidentiality.* No one should repeat what someone shares in the group unless that person gives permission. Even then, discretion is imperative. Since this study deals with overcoming fears and the discussion of personal experiences, it is essential that group members trust each other. Participants should talk about their own feelings and experiences, not those of others.

▼ *Attendance.* Each session builds on the previous ones, and you need continuity from each other.

Ask group members to commit to attending all six sessions, unless an emergency arises.
▼ *Participation.* If the study guide is used without a main lecture on each topic, the sessions will focus on group discussion. It is important that each person be given an opportunity to participate if she desires to do so.
▼ *Honesty.* Appropriate openness is a key to a good group. Be who you really are, not who you think you ought to be.

The purpose of the warm-up is to get acquainted and establish a friendly atmosphere for subsequent discussions. As you begin a new study, it is helpful to give women a chance to get to know each other and to create a "risk-free" environment. The warm-up will be the most successful if you go first, modeling openness and brevity. Try not to spend more than ten minutes on this exercise so that you will have plenty of time for the rest of your discussion.

Have women take turns reading the text portions of the study aloud. Discuss questions as you go. Text will be sprinkled throughout all six sessions with discussion questions intermingled. Assign different people to read specific sections, or for variety, have the group read some silently. You will need to move the discussion from one question to the next before all possible discussion has been exhausted in order to get through the material within ninety minutes. Alternatively, you can select among the questions those that seem most important.

In chapters 1 and 2 of the book *Tame Your Fears*, there is a complete explanation of the chain reaction whereby we choose a destructive or a constructive resolution for our fears. You will find it helpful to read the relevant chapters in the book for a clear personal understanding of the subject, so you can better explain it to the class.

On page 11 and on page 91 there is a diagram of the chain reaction that will be discussed in each session. Be sure to refer to it during the first few sessions to clarify the process of resolving our fears. If you are presenting a lecture on this material in front of a large audience, limited permission is given to enlarge the diagram on page 91 to prepare an overhead transparency for your use while teaching this material. Many people in every audience are visual thinkers who understand the subject more easily if they can picture it in their minds.

Be sure to study the discussion questions ahead of time and mark those that are less essential for your group, in case you run short of time. Since the needs of women differ greatly from group to group, you will be the best judge of which questions could most easily be omitted.

Perhaps most important of all is to allow time to pray together at the end of the discussion. Each session has a "Looking to God" section with a suggestion for prayer related to the topic covered in the study. At the end of this first session, you could keep the group together for prayer. Have any volunteers offer a sentence or two of thanksgiving to the Lord for recent answers to prayer. Ask each woman to pray silently for the woman on her right, then for the woman on her left. Ask the women to share silently with God a fear they have experienced within the last few weeks or months. Encourage them to ask Him to help them choose a constructive resolution for their fear based on the truth of His Word, not on their emotions of the moment. Pray that the whole group will have the courage to face their fears honestly.

As the leader, you should close in prayer, asking God to meet the specific need of every participant in the group.

During this first meeting, some women may be afraid to come back if they think you will randomly call on them to pray aloud. Therefore, it's helpful to have volunteers be the only ones who pray aloud during this beginning session. (If your group is totally made up of "seasoned saints," modify these instructions to fit the spiritual maturity of the group.)

Following prayer, take a few minutes to refer to the "Into Our Lives" section. Give a brief overview of the content and suggest that participants go through this section on their own during the week to reinforce and put into practice what they are learning. Tell the women this exercise will take some tough thinking and time. Remind them that we often "bury" our fears through denial, defeat, bitterness, or escape, and it has taken many of us *years* to get in touch with these deep emotions. End with a positive personal statement regarding the spiritual benefit of coming to grips with our fearful emotions.

Encourage members of the group to memorize the suggested verse (or verses) in the "For Memorization" section. During the warm-up in subsequent weeks, ask if anyone would like to recite a key verse from the previous week.

TIPS FOR LEADING A DISCUSSION

Work toward a relaxed and open atmosphere. This may not come quickly, so as the leader you must model acceptance, openness to truth and change, and love. Develop a genuine interest in each person's remarks, and expect to learn from each of them. Show that you care by listening carefully. Be affirming. Sometimes a hug is the best response.

Pay attention to how you ask questions. Don't ask, "What did you get for questions 1? Instead, by your tone of voice convey (1) your interest and enthusiasm for the question and (2) your warmth toward the group. The group will adopt your attitude.

Because of the highly personal nature of a study involving the sharing of paralyzing fears, just listening to other group members may be total participation for some women who are too close to a personal fear to talk about it yet.

Ask only one question at a time. Often, participants' responses will suggest a follow-up question to you. Be discerning as to when you are following a fruitful train of thought and when you are going on a tangent.

Be aware of time. Don't spend so much time discussing that you run out of time for prayer. Your goal is not to have something to discuss, but to become more like Jesus Christ.

Encourage constructive controversy. The group can learn a lot from struggling with the many sides of an issue. If you aren't threatened when someone disagrees, the whole group will be more open and vulnerable. Intervene, when necessary, making sure that people debate ideas and interpretations of Scripture, not attack each other's feelings or character. If the group gets stuck in an unresolvable argument, say something like, "We can agree to disagree here," and move on.

Don't be the expert. People will stop contributing if they think that you are judging their answers or that you think you know best. Let the Bible be the expert—the final say. Let the members candidly express their feelings and experiences.

Don't do for the group what it can do for itself. With a beginning group, you may have to ask all of the questions and do all of the planning, but within a few meetings you should start delegating various leadership responsibilities. Help members learn to exercise their gifts. Let them start making decisions and solving problems together. Encourage them to maturity and unity in Christ.

Summarize the discussion frequently. Summarizing what has been said will help the group see where the discussion is going.

Let the group plan applications. The group and individual action responses in the "Into Our Lives" sections are suggestions. Your group should adapt these ideas to be relevant and life-changing for the members. If group members aren't committed to an application, they won't do it. Encourage, but don't force.

End your meetings with refreshments. Having coffee or soft drinks plus a small snack gives people an excuse to stay for a few extra minutes and discuss the subject informally. Often the most life-changing decisions and conversations occur after the formal session.

The topic of this study may attract nonChristians who are curious about what the Bible says about dealing with fear. Be alert. Don't be surprised if you get the awesome opportunity of leading someone to Christ!

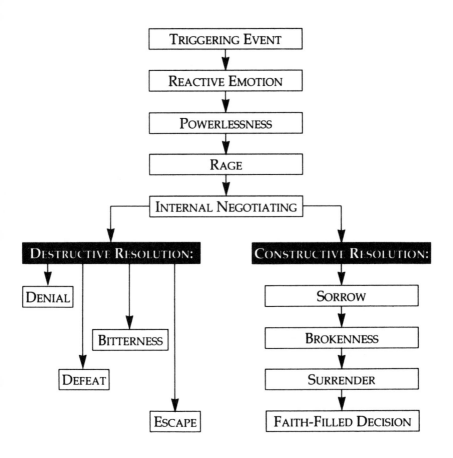